BARRON'S

Immanuel Birmelin

My Parakeet
and Me

Photographs: Monika Wegler
Illustrations: Renate Holzner

Table of Contents

Typical Parakeets

Golden Rules for Proper Care

take care

watch it

Building Trust from the Start

love it

Parakeet Stories

Fun and Games with Parakeets

have fun

Active and Happy in Old Age

old & happy

Golden

Parakeets are skillful and eager fliers.
For this reason, a pet parakeet absolutely must
have a period of free flight every day. Other
basic requirements for a healthy parakeet include
a properly equipped cage, a healthy diet,
and the right kind of routine care.

Rules

for Proper Care

The 10 Golden Rules for Equipment

1 For two parakeets, the cage should be at least 28 inches (70 cm) long, 16 inches (40 cm) wide, and 20 inches (50 cm) high.

2 Choose a cage with horizontal bars that are not coated with plastic.

3 Cage doors that open out and down serve as a platform for takeoff and landing.

4 Perches should be made of wood. Branches of varying diameter provide exercise for the bird's feet.

5 Feed dishes, an automatic water dispenser, and a whetstone for the beak are essential items in every cage.

6 Parakeets love swings, ladders, or rings to play on. Small branches and twigs from willow, oak, alder, poplar, mountain ash, and fruit trees also provide entertainment.

7 To keep your feathered friends from getting bored, give them a few toys at a time and change the selection often. (Some parakeets may prefer the same "love object" and are frightened of new toys.)

8 Put some bird sand in a cup attached to the cage.

9 Place the cage where the birds have a high vantage point, as birds are especially fearful of danger that strikes from above.

10 A bird tree made of natural branches will soon become a favorite spot for your bird during its free flight.

The
10 Golden
Rules for
Feeding

1 Parakeets need fresh water every day, along with seeds and grains, fresh greens, fruit, and vegetables. Every two to three days, offer a spray of millet.

2 Seed mixtures that have passed their expiration date contain hardly any vitamins.

3 Introduce greens, fruit, and vegetables when your parakeets are 8 to 16 weeks old.

4 Cut fruits and vegetables into small pieces. Wash greens with warm water and air dry.

5 Every evening, remove wilted greens and spoiled fruit and vegetables.

6 Whole plants, including the root, aid digestion. (Try dandelions and shepherd's purse.)

7 Divide the day's food into separate feedings, for example in the morning and the late afternoon.

8 Provide a mineral block that contains iodine at all times and give a multivitamin preparation in winter.

9 When your bird is molting (losing its feathers and growing new ones), consider a special supplement (sold in pet stores).

10 Beware of poisonous plants and fruits, such as avocado, ivy, yew, and daffodil.

The 10 Golden Rules for Care

1 Clean the feed and water containers daily. Spoiled food is a breeding ground for bacteria, viruses, and fungi.

2 Scrub the cage and all the equipment once a week with hot water.

3 Replace the bird sand as it becomes soiled. Change it completely at least once a week.

4 Replace the branches and twigs in the cage and in the room at regular intervals.

5 Parakeets love to bathe and splash. Hang a bathhouse in the cage door now and then.

6 Make sure your bird can fly freely about the room for at least two hours every day, but do not leave it unattended.

7 When your bird is molting, remove the dropped feathers several times a week.

8 If the bird's beak and claws grow too long, take it to the veterinarian to have them trimmed.

9 Female parakeets have a strong need to gnaw. Be sure they have plenty of branches, some grit, and a whetstone.

10 Spend plenty of time playing and talking with your feathered friends.

Typical

Oscar, Goldi, and Frankie have just enjoyed a flight around the room, while Mimi chose to stay in the cage. This little colony of parakeets gets along very well. They never quarrel—they even share a millet spray in peace. Gregarious by nature, parakeets need the company of others of their species.

Parakeets

Small Parrots from Australia

Parakeets are vividly colored and lively parrots whose homeland is Australia. No other bird species in the world has as many color variants and combinations as the parakeet. The pet parakeets that flutter about your house may be cobalt blue, yellow, or even a bluish gray—indeed, almost any color except red and black. Parakeets may be pied or almost uniform in hue. But this was not always the case. The wide variety of coloration developed only after humans began to collect and breed parakeets, some 150 years ago. Wild parakeets in Australia, the forebears of all our variously colored pets, have green feathers.

Life in the Flock

In their native habitat, parakeets live in colonies, where each bird is one among many. There are no dominant males or females, no disputes over a female or a prime feeding spot. This natural heritage gives our pet parakeets their peaceful dispositions. They need other parakeets for company, so it's best to keep more than one.

Within the flock, a parakeet may live as an individual or may choose a mate.

Living as a colony helps parakeets to survive in the hot, dry climate of their homeland. When one of these fleet and nimble bundles of energy finds a source of food or water, the whole flock follows.

In the wild, parakeets have green feathers. This offers protective coloration in their native habitat.

An Outdoor Escapade

Lilly and Billy, our parakeets, enjoy free flight about the room for several hours every day. During this time, I'm very careful to keep all the doors and windows closed. But one day, Billy was too quick for me. As I left the room, he darted through the door and down the hall behind me. Before I knew it, he had followed me out the back door into the garden. Quick as a wink, he flew to the top of a nearby pine tree.

How could I entice him back into the house? One option was to tempt him with a tasty snack. Another possibility was to take advantage of his attachment to Lilly, his mate. Quickly, I fetched an old cage from the cellar, set it on the patio, and placed a sprig of millet spray inside, leaving the cage door open. Then I put Lilly back in her cage, closed the door securely, and brought her outdoors, setting the cage on the patio beside the other one. Soon Lilly began to call to her mate, just as parakeets do in the wild to maintain contact with others in the flock. It seemed that my strategy just might work.

Sure enough, after an hour or so, Billy flew from the pine tree to the patio to reassure his mate. Before very long, he noticed the millet spray in the adjacent cage, and he couldn't resist. When he hopped inside to satisfy his hunger, I gently closed the door behind him. Soon the adventurer and his mate were back in the safety of their indoor home.

BILLY + LILLY

As many as a thousand birds may throng to one small thicket or water hole, where they all eat and drink together. They perch on branches or stalks of grass, cracking the grains with their beaks, or peck at ripe seeds on the ground. If one bird flies off to another feeding spot, the others will call him back or follow as a group. They like to have company while they eat—and there is safety in numbers. They can warn each other if danger threatens, and a predator finds it hard to single out a single bird.

➡ For happy parakeets: Give your bird plenty of fresh fruits and vegetables that are pesticide free. Check with your veterinarian about those to avoid.

Parakeets Aren't Good Singles

Too often, parakeets live as household pets in solitary confinement. Why does this happen? Many parakeet owners believe that if they keep several birds, the flock won't become tame; others think that their single parakeet is doing fine. In each case, they are badly mistaken, as scientific studies have shown. The studies compared the behavior of solitary parakeets with that of those living in groups. Young birds that have lived alone in a cage for three months are louder and more timid, showing almost no interest in their surroundings. They sing and warble for hours on end, like lonely people talking to themselves. Their anxiety also affects their social behavior.

What Parakeets Are Like

➡ The parakeet is a small member of the parrot family. Its native habitat is Australia. Wild parakeets live in flocks.

➡ Their strong, curved beak is a useful tool, especially for gnawing on wood.

➡ Their feet are ideally shaped for grasping and climbing. (Two toes point forward and two point backward.)

➡ Like many parrots, they can learn to talk.

➡ Parakeets are easily tamed.

➡ Parrots are lively and affectionate pets. Once a parakeet becomes your friend, it will remain devoted to you for the rest of its life.

➡ Mother parakeets help their chicks to hatch from the egg.

➡ As birds go, they are endurance athletes. Parakeets can fly at high speed for long distances.

➡ They are very inquisitive and love to play games.

➡ Wild parakeets weigh about 1 ounce (30 g), their domesticated cousins 1.2 to 1.4 ounces (35–40 g).

➡ Parakeets are sexually mature at three months old.

When they encounter a parakeet they don't know, they either cower from it or threaten it. By contrast, parakeets that live in company with others approach the strange parakeet to make friendly contact.

➔ For happy parakeets: Never keep a parakeet by itself. Two tame birds will bring you more pleasure.

Finding the Right Partner

Parakeets are charming couples, forming bonds that last a lifetime. Parakeets begin to seek a mate very early in life—as young as a few months old. But how do they identify the right partner? Do they go strictly by outer appearances, or is it possible that feelings also matter? We don't know for certain, but we do know that females prefer older males, and young males prefer females who are in possession of a nesting box (nesting cavity). Then are these pairings

just a matter of practicality? Not entirely. Those who have watched parakeets for many years have noticed that certain pairs are more affectionate than others. They spend more time together, billing and cooing and scratching each other's heads. It seems clear that parakeets also have their personal preferences.

➔ For happy parakeets: Purchase two birds that get along well together. This is a much more important consideration than the color of their feathers (see the *Parakeet Story* on page 20).

Even birds of the same sex, like these two males, can sometimes become fast friends.

TIP from the BREEDER

Purchase young parakeets, five to six weeks of age. At this age, the birds adjust most readily to you and their new home (see page 32). Young parakeets have large, black, shoe-button eyes, with the white iris not yet visible.

Baby Birds on the Way

Many parakeet owners worry that their birds will produce offspring whether the owners are ready or not. However, this is most unlikely. To reproduce, parakeets need not only plenty of food and water, but in most cases also a suitable nesting box or cavity. The darkness in the nesting cavity stimulates the hormones the female needs for her eggs to mature. Without this darkness, there generally won't be any eggs.

Before the female parakeet is ready to mate, the male must put her in the mood with his courtship rituals. To woo his chosen mate, he feeds her with seeds regurgitated from his crop. If the female is receptive, she stands still, with her head thrown back, head feathers plumped up, and tail raised high. This posture signals to the male that she is ready and willing. The male then climbs on the female's back, folding one or both wings about her in a protective gesture as they mate.

What about parakeet pairs that do not have a nesting box? Are they discontented? Presumably not; many a male woos his partner and mates with her even if no nesting cavity is available. Biologists formerly had difficulty explaining such supposedly useless mating behavior. Now that they are willing to admit that animals have feelings, they have an easier time of it. Why shouldn't parakeets enjoy the mating act?

Busy Parents at Work

The mating period and the search for a nest go hand in hand. It's the female's job to find a suitable nesting cavity. After the mother-to-be has laid her eggs, the male is her only contact with the outside world. He brings food to his mate and, later, to the baby birds. The female lays four to six eggs, two days apart, on the floor of the nesting box. Laying the eggs takes all her strength. Only after the last egg is laid does she have a chance to rest as she broods the eggs. She sits on them to keep them warm, turns them at regular intervals, and leaves the clutch only to defecate some distance away.

➜ For happy parakeets: Don't let your birds breed more than twice a year; otherwise, the female may die of exhaustion. To prevent them from breeding again, just before the chicks leave the nesting box (when they are about four weeks old) you should separate the parents and remove the nesting box.

The Chicks Hatch

After about 17 days, the time arrives. The first chick peeps to its mother from inside the egg. Why does it do this? It is preparing the mother parakeet for its imminent arrival. Without these appealing pleas for her attention and care, the mother might reject the hatchling as an intruder when it finally appears. The chick communicates with its mother in this way for about a day before it begins to work its way out of the shell. With its egg tooth, a small sharp projection on its soft bill, it begins to chip at the shell. Turning within the membrane that surrounds it, it punches hole after hole—rather like a can opener—until it has created an opening. Finally, peeping loudly, it pushes its way into the world.

Almost all birds are merely spectators as their chicks hatch. It does not occur to them to help their offspring with the strenuous effort involved, even if the chick is too weak to crack the tough shell on its own.

Not so the parakeets. If such a crisis occurs, the mother parakeet comes to her chick's rescue. Bit by bit, she chips away at the shell, helping the chick to create a good-sized opening. She continues to peck away until she has reached the egg membrane, which she eagerly nibbles at. Even when the hatchling is free of the shell, the mother parakeet pays it no attention until she has completely broken up the shell and consumed the entire membrane. But how does the mother bird know that she must help her baby? Does she understand what she is doing?

No, not exactly; she is acting instinctively, in response to a number of stimuli. The chick's

Release your parakeets to fly freely about the room for several hours every day.

Romeo and Juliet

My daughter longed to have a parakeet.
Finally, in the local pet store, we found the
bird of her dreams—a jaunty male with bril-
liant green plumage. Beside him was a female,
plain bluish gray. We could tell that the two
birds liked each other; they sat close together
on the perch, billing and cooing and preening each
other's feathers. But we didn't want two parakeets—
just the handsome male, whom my daughter immediately
named Buster. A good-sized cage was ready and waiting
at home, so the friendly saleswoman took Buster from
the aviary and placed him in a small cardboard box
for us. We took him straight home and released him
into his gleaming new cage—a palace fit for a prince.
We were sure he would enjoy having all that space to
himself, with no other birds claiming their turn at
the feed dish or the cute little swing. But instead,
Buster huddled by himself in a corner of the cage. He
wasn't even interested in eating. What could have
transformed our once-perky parakeet into this forlorn
creature?

Finally, my daughter had an idea. She remembered
the bluish-gray female at the pet store. Could
Buster be pining for his mate? We hurried back to
the pet store, bought the little female, and
brought her home. When we placed her in the cage,
we could hardly believe our eyes. The
two parakeets snuggled close together,
twittering with pleasure and nibbling
tenderly at each other with their
beaks. After some time, they began
to explore their new home, finally
settling down together to share a
millet spray. My daughter named the
little female Juliet, and our
lonely Buster is now a happy Romeo.

desperate struggle and the hole appearing in the shell impel the mother parakeet to peck and chip as she does.

But why do mother parakeets respond differently than other parent birds? The answer lies in the harsh climatic conditions of their native Australia. Because the parakeet's natural habitat is very hot and dry, the moisture within the egg sac evaporates rapidly. If the hatchling doesn't escape from the shell quickly, the membrane that surrounds it will adhere to it and prevent it from turning within the shell. The chick will not be able to peck the circle of holes that creates an opening through which it can emerge on its own. Without its mother's help, the chick would be trapped in the shell and die.

Not all hatchlings need this assistance, of course. In captivity, this behavior occurs only about a third of the time.

The hatchlings are blind, naked, and help-less, but within about four weeks their feathers are fully grown. At this point, the fledglings look almost exactly like the adult birds, although their eyes are still relatively large and uniformly dark, with no iris ring. The feather markings on their head look like little waves, and their cere (the nostril area above the beak) has not changed color. Later, the cere of the male will turn blue, and females have a brownish cere.

Within three months, the parakeet grows from a tiny creature weighing less than a tenth of an ounce (2 g) to an adult bird that is ready to have babies of its own. Until then, however, the juveniles are still fed by their parents.

The Senses

Vision: For parakeets, as for humans, the eyes are probably the most important sense organs. But how and what they see is very different. Parakeets are swift fliers, and they must be able

Six weeks old, this young parakeet nestles trustingly in a quiet hand.

to spot a predator instantly. Their eyes can process as many as 150 images per second—nearly ten times as many as the human eye. But what does this mean? Think of it this way: a movie or television program would seem as slow to a parakeet as a boring slide show does to you. A parakeet's eyes are located on the sides of its head, providing an almost panoramic field of vision. Even enemies approaching it from behind are quickly detected. The disadvantage of this eye position is that depth perception is diminished. Essentially, a parakeet sees a flat image of the world, as we do when we close one eye. On the other hand, its world is probably more colorful than ours, for parakeets have four types of sensory cells in their eyes, while we have only three. The fourth type of cell can absorb UV rays from sunlight.

Smell and taste: Parakeets probably don't have a highly developed sense of smell. On the other hand, their

sense of taste is fairly good. A parakeet has about 350 taste buds, while a human has 9,000. We know that parakeets can distinguish sweet, sour, salty, and bitter flavors.

Hearing: Parakeets hear sounds in the frequency range from 400 to 20,000 hertz (humans from 16 to 20,000 hertz). They don't hear deep tones at all, and it's questionable whether shrill sounds bother them the way they do humans. What is remarkable about a parakeet's hearing is its ability to recognize and remember specific sequences of notes. In the wild, this skill is essential for communication and survival. Certain calls, especially the shrill alarm signal, must be repeated exactly to carry the intended meaning. A noise that sounds like a long loud shriek to the human ear is recognizable to the parakeet as a distinct sequence of notes. This may explain why a parakeet will fly into a panic at certain sounds that seem perfectly harmless to us.

These two perky cocks seem totally relaxed in the presence of a dwarf rabbit.

Feeling: With special sense cells in their legs and elsewhere, birds are highly sensitive to vibrations.

➜ For happy parakeets: Be sure to place the birdcage well away from any sources of vibration (such as the refrigerator motor) that will cause your parakeets stress.

Typical Behavior

The way animals behave gives us information about their perceptions, feelings, intelligence, and ability to learn. Many abilities and characteristics are inherited; others are acquired during the animal's life. As a result, each animal has its own personality and talents. Here are some of the things you may see your parakeet do.

Flapping its wings: Grasping the perch or the bars of the cage securely with its feet, the bird flaps its wings vigorously without actually taking flight. Young parakeets do this to exercise their muscles, but if your adult parakeet does this, it probably needs more time for free flight outside the cage.

Preening its feathers: Because clean feathers are essential for optimal efficiency in flight, parakeets spend a good deal of time each day grooming their feathers. The bird draws each flight feather on the wings and tail through its beak. It also uses its feet to clean the area around its cloaca (anal aperture).

TIP from the VETERINARIAN

Perches of different diameters exercise the bird's foot muscles. Perches that have diameters of the same size can strain the bird's feet because of the bird's inability to exercise different muscles. Proper perches are made of nontoxic hardwood.

Mutual grooming and nibbling: This social behavior is like a massage for the birds. The parakeets nibble on their partner's head feathers, not only to help clean them, but as a way of bonding.

Resting: The parakeet sits still, with its feathers plumped up. The eyes are usually closed, and one leg is tucked up close to the body. If your bird seems to be spending more time than usual in this position, it may be sick or lonely. Parakeets usually alternate between rest and activity; the active periods should be longer than the rest periods.

Sleeping: Sitting on its perch, the bird turns its head and tucks it under its ruffled back feathers, eyes closed. One foot may be drawn up under the belly feathers. Could the parakeet be dreaming of happy adventures? It's quite possible. French scientists have observed signs of dreaming in birds, and we know that baby chickens dream. Leave your parakeet to dream in peace; if you wake it up, it might panic. If a parakeet sleeps almost all day long, however, it is probably sick.

Courtship feeding: The male feeds the female with food regurgitated from its crop. To do this, the two birds hook their beaks together at a right angle. A parakeet kept as a solitary pet might do the same thing with an object or even a person, but this is not natural behavior.

Aggression: The parakeet attacks another bird, snapping at it with its beak and sometimes striking out with one foot. The aggressor may make an "Ihh" sound at the same time. If two of your parakeets fight often, you must separate them.

Gnawing: Females in a broody mood will gnaw on almost everything. Be sure to provide them with plenty of twigs and branches.

Singing: When parakeets sing, they plump up their feathers and sometimes close their eyes. This warbling and trilling is a sign that they are healthy and happy.

Alarm call: A short, shrill call.

Screeching from loneliness: Parakeets that are separated from the flock or from their mate emit a clear shrill call again and again.

Billing: Two parakeets hook their beaks together at a right angle. This is an expression of tenderness.

Frankie loves to nibble on the vitamin-rich greens, also known as "cat grass."

How Well Do You Know Your Parakeets?

The first step to taking good care of your parakeets is learning about their behavior and their needs. Here's a little quiz to see how much you already know about these perky little parrots. The answers are given below—but no peeking!

	YES	NO
1 Does a parakeet need a companion?	◯	◯
2 Do parakeets see the world in brighter colors than we do?	◯	◯
3 Do most parakeets live to be more than 20 years old?	◯	◯
4 Does a pair of parakeets separate when the birds grow old?	◯	◯
5 Do parakeets have a keen sense of smell?	◯	◯
6 Do female parakeets have a brownish cere (skin patch above the beak)?	◯	◯
7 In the wild, do parakeets live in flocks?	◯	◯
8 Can all parakeets learn to talk?	◯	◯
9 Can parakeets reproduce even if a nesting box is not available?	◯	◯
10 Do both the father and the mother parakeet care for the young?	◯	◯
11 Do parakeets often fight with each other?	◯	◯
12 Does the mother parakeet help a chick to hatch from the egg?	◯	◯

Answers: 1 = yes; 2 = yes; 3 = no; 4 = no; 5 = no; 6 = yes; 7 = yes; 8 = no; 9 = yes; 10 = yes; 11 = no; 12 = yes.

Building

Pepper loves his human family almost as much as he loves his mate Honey. As soon as the cage door opens, he zips into the air and around the room a few times, scolding with shrill cries if nobody holds a finger out for him to land on. He enjoys being carried around to see the sights, or having a little chat with a familiar person.

Trust
from the Start

love it

TIP from the THERAPIST

When you purchase your parakeets, you should bring them home by the shortest route. Right away, give them a millet spray to nibble on. The tasty treat will help the parakeets to develop a positive attitude toward their new surroundings.

Understanding a Parakeet's Feelings

Your very first interactions with your parakeets will determine whether your birds will learn to trust you or will always be timid. Many bird owners have a hard time imagining what their new little neighbors are going through as they adjust to an unfamiliar place, because they don't understand how the birds feel. It might be easier to sympathize if we look at the situation in human terms. Imagine a little girl who lives in an orphanage or children's home. It may take her a while to learn the routine and begin to make friends, but after a while she feels pretty comfortable. Suddenly, she is moved from the orphanage to live with foster parents. Even though they are kind and caring, and do everything they can to make her welcome, it's very likely that she will cry at first and feel sad and lonely.

What does this story have to do with our small feathered friends? Of course, a parakeet isn't human, and its feelings aren't as profound. Nevertheless, it too feels fear and loneliness. At the breeder's or at the pet store, it lives with a flock of young comrades. One day, without warning, it is taken from the flock and shut up in a small dark box. This experience is a shock for the little parakeet. Although a well-equipped birdcage awaits it, everything about its new home is unfamiliar. It will need time to adjust. You will have to exercise a great deal of patience, care, and sympathy while the parakeet learns to trust you and feel comfortable in its new environment.

Be very gentle as you welcome these new members of your household. The time you invest now will pay off later. A parakeet that is tamed to your touch not only brings you a good deal of pleasure, but also saves a lot of effort. To give just one example, consider how much more stressful it is for both bird and human when an untamed parakeet must be caught and put back in the cage after its period of free flight—which it must have every day if it is to thrive.

Give your feathered friends plenty of time to explore their new surroundings. Don't rush them. Let *them* set the pace.

Tips for the Adjustment Period

There are a few essential rules to keep in mind as your new parakeets begin to settle in.

First of all, try not to point your finger at parakeets; this can frighten them badly. Oftentimes parakeets will flee from a pointing finger. Why is this? We don't really know. Perhaps it looks to them like the beak of a hawk or other bird of prey.

On the other hand, clicking sounds and soft words calm the birds, reduce their fear of humans, and help to build trust. In the wild, parakeets must always be alert for possible danger, and their instinctive response is to take flight. Fear is a natural part of their makeup. And yet, fear can also inhibit their curiosity and, over time, diminish their sense of well-being. Therefore, you must make a conscious effort to keep your small, lonely, defenseless parakeet from feeling afraid. But how? Here are a few tips: Avoid shrill sounds and rapid movements. Don't slam the door, and don't suddenly turn bright lights on or off. Even an unexpected change in your appearance —a new hat, sunglasses, rollers in your hair— can alarm your parakeet. Finally, never take hold of your parakeet from above. It would feel as if it were being seized by a bird of prey, and it would be terrified.

Your Parakeets' Wish List

What parakeets like:

1. Parakeets enjoy listening to quiet music.

2. Female parakeets like to nibble on the corners of wooden objects.

3. All parakeets relish a sunbath or a rain shower.

4. At midday, they like to nap in a spot that's sunny, but not too hot.

5. Parakeets need plenty of fresh air that's rich in oxygen.

6. Birds need grit to aid the digestive process.

7. Without ample time for free flight every day, parakeets will not thrive.

What parakeets don't like:

1. Parakeets are gregarious, and don't like being alone.

2. Shrill sounds and sudden loud noises bother them.

3. Absolute silence makes parakeets nervous.

4. Glaring light and rapid hand movements disturb them.

5. Unexpected changes in your appearance, like a new hat or hairdo, will alarm your parakeets.

6. Very high temperatures (above 86°F, 30°C) and stale indoor air make them uncomfortable.

7. Avoid drafts; the parakeets might catch cold.

8. They don't like being grabbed in your hand or tossed into the air.

9. Parakeets don't like foods that taste sour.

Children and Parakeets

Animals are especially fascinating to young children. Why is this?

Children are naturally curious. They respond instinctively to parakeets, guinea pigs, and other small animals. Again and again, I notice how differently adults and children react when they first see the 24 parakeets in my aviary. The children stand wide-eyed, captivated by the throng of brightly colored birds. They watch the parakeets intently. After a few minutes, they may have identified the ones that are pairs. They ask questions like, "Why do some of the birds have brown noses and others have blue ones?" Adults ask quite different questions: "How often do you have to clean the cages? What do the parakeets eat?"

On the other hand, children have very little grasp of the amount of work involved in taking care of a pet. Parents must teach their children not only what a parakeet needs, but also why. As children learn how to feed the birds, give them fresh water, and keep their cage clean, they also are learning to take responsibility for the well-being of another living creature. As they learn to approach the parakeets quietly, give them a safe space to fly freely, and interpret their warbles and trills, they also are learning how to understand their needs and feelings. This sympathetic understanding of another creature—whether it's an animal or a person—is a component of social intelligence. The habits a child learns while caring for a pet may later contribute to teamwork in the family or the workplace.

Keep in mind that parakeets are not suitable pets for children under 10 years old. Young children have a tremendous need for physical contact—touching, holding, cuddling. Parakeets, however, dislike and fear such contact. Only in rare cases will they tolerate being petted. Furthermore, small children have not yet developed full motor skills. Their sudden and uncontrolled movements alarm the birds. Older children, by contrast, can take pleasure in simply watching the parakeets. They also are capable of understanding and meeting the birds' needs.

A tame parakeet may enjoy being scratched gently on its belly.

Goldi's Adventures

Goldi is one of the funniest parakeets I know. Comical adventures seem to follow him around. For example, the other day he was flitting about the room as usual when he spied the sugar bowl. The silver spoon particularly drew his attention, because parakeets love shiny objects. In a flash, he had landed on the handle of the spoon. To his astonishment, his weight flipped the spoon into the air, and he was showered with sugar!

But Goldi is naturally inquisitive, so he continued his exploration of the tea table. Next, he encountered a dish of lemon slices. Of course, he had to nibble at one—and the resulting pucker on his little face made it clear that the sour taste did not agree with him at all.

Even that experience didn't daunt my brave explorer. He hopped jauntily along the table to a glass of carbonated water. Perching on the edge of the glass, he dipped his beak in for a drink. But the tiny bubbles rising in the glass and bursting on the surface were too much for him. He shook his head vigorously in obvious distaste.

More often than not, my funny little friend learns from his adventures. I love to tell the story of his first "piano lesson." One day, someone left the piano lid open, and Goldi happened to land on the keys, bringing forth a tuneless tumble of notes. With a squawk of dismay, he fled to the safety of his cage—and from then on, on his daily outings, he gives the piano a wide berth.

← GOLDI

Building Trust Step by Step

When you bring a new parakeet home, your main goal for the first few weeks should be to help it get used to its new surroundings and to you.

During this time, make every effort to avoid alarming the bird in any way (see page 29). Whenever you are nearby, talk softly to your parakeet, and call it by name. Bring food and fresh water at the same time each morning and afternoon; your parakeet will appreciate the predictability of this regular schedule. Move gently and quietly, so as not to startle it.

Avoid Stress

To tame your parakeet to your touch, you must be very sensitive to its feelings. Never grab it and hold it; this would frighten it badly. And a hold that is too tight may inadvertently prevent the parakeet from breathing. Instead, wait until your parakeet is comfortable just having you nearby. This could take several days; be patient. Then follow the steps outlined on the next pages, and again, take your time. Don't move from one step to the next until you're sure the parakeet is ready.

Your parakeet will learn to trust you, but only if you give it plenty of time.

1 Arouse Its Curiosity

At first, approach the cage only when the door is closed and the parakeet is resting on its perch. Avoid shrill noises and sudden movement. If the parakeet shrinks away as you draw near, stop where you are for a while, then try again. If it stays on its perch, stand so that your face is level with the parakeet and talk quietly to it. This will arouse its curiosity.

2 A Peace Offering

Now open the cage door with one hand. In the other hand, hold out a tasty treat, such as a millet spray. The parakeet will watch your movements carefully, but most of its attention will be on the snack in your hand. Keep talking softly to your pet. Give the parakeet time to gather its courage and come closer.

3 The Moment of Truth

Wait until the parakeet hops onto the millet spray in your hand. Try not to make any noises that would startle the bird. While it nibbles on the treat, draw your hand away from the cage and toward you—very slowly, inch by inch, so the bird doesn't notice. Then hold still and let the parakeet eat. After a few moments, gently and slowly move your hand back into the cage. Wait until the parakeet hops off, then close the door. Well done!

4 Your Parakeet Goes Exploring

Remove the parakeet from the cage as described in step 3. After a while, it may hop onto your hand and venture up your forearm, exploring. Carefully rest your arm on the table, then lay your head down as well. Watch and wait. Soon, the parakeet will hop up by your ear and start to nibble on your hair—a favorite trick of most parakeets.

5 Now the Ice Is Broken

Your feathered friend is learning to trust you and gaining the courage to explore its surroundings. Keep its attention by giving it things to gnaw on—a newspaper, an old calendar, a knobby branch, a small block of wood. Stay near your pet, and keep talking softly while it hops around.

6 Completely Relaxed

No longer timid and shy, your parakeet is now a lively comrade. The bond between you is so strong that your pet feels comfortable playing while you look on. This is a sign of great trust, because birds will not play unless they are completely relaxed and free of any fear. From now on, give your feathered friend plenty of opportunities to play like this.

How Did Mike and Mitzi Become a Pair?

Mike was a solitary parakeet, and he obviously wasn't happy about it. His owners decided to provide him with a partner, a female they named Mitzi. But parakeets are individuals, and two birds won't necessarily get along right away. Here's how to give them a good start:

➜ Put each bird in its own cage, and place the cages in different rooms.

➜ After both birds are tame to your touch, set the two cages side by side.

➜ When the birds begin to warble to each other and bill and coo through the bars, open the cage doors and let them both fly about the room, while you watch.

➜ In most cases, they will get along fine. When they are tired of flying, they will settle down together happily—like Mike and Mitzi.

Compatibility Test

	Parakeet	Cockatiel	Lovebird	Parrot	Guinea Pig	Rat	Dog	Cat
Parakeet	❤	❤❤	≋	💣	≋	💣	☺	💣
Cockatiel	❤❤	❤	❤❤	💣	≋	💣	☺	💣
Lovebird	≋	❤❤	❤	☺	≋	💣	☺	💣
Parrot	💣	💣	☺	❤	≋	💣	☺	💣
Guinea Pig	≋	≋	≋	≋	❤	☺	☺	💣
Rat	💣	💣	💣	💣	☺	❤	☺	💣
Dog	☺	☺	☺	☺	☺	☺	≋	☺
Cat	💣	💣	💣	💣	💣	💣	☺	☺

❤ *Get along best*   💣 *A deadly combination*   ≋ *Indifferent to each other*   ☺ *Can learn to get along*

Any books that you care about are best kept out of your parakeets' reach.

Free Flight About the Room

Parakeets need several hours of free flight every day if they are to thrive. The exercise strengthens their muscles and keeps their heart and circulatory system fit.

In the wild, parakeets are strong and skilled fliers. They can reach speeds of up to 75 miles (120 kilometers) per hour, and they may fly for hours on end in search of food or water. They are amazingly nimble in flight; the entire flock can change its direction at once, even at breakneck speed, much as swallows do.

Before you release your parakeet for its first flight, it should be tame to your hand (see page 32). Then you will have no difficulty luring it to your hand with a spray of millet so that you can put it back in the cage when the time comes. Surprisingly, many parakeets must be coaxed from the cage for the first flight. Apparently they are reluctant to leave the safety of their familiar home. Here, too, a millet spray resting on the open cage door will serve as enticement.

At the mirror **1**

What's this? Another parakeet? Frankie tries hard to make friends with his image in the mirror, while Max looks on in bemusement.

2 On the potted palm

From this vantage point, Oscar has a great view. What's more, the palm leaves make pretty tasty nibbling.

3 At the jewelry box

Here's a treasure trove of toys. But be careful—certain jewelry items can be toxic to your bird.

4 On the hand

Max likes this perch best, and he would never refuse a tender leaf of lettuce.

5 Thirst

Several tours around the room can make a fellow thirsty.

6 An indoor playground

Pet stores sell swings and ladders that provide good fun for a parakeet.

Safety Checklist

➔ Keep doors and windows closed. (The parakeet might fly away.)

➔ Hang curtains at bare windowpanes, or apply decals. (The bird might crash into the glass.)

➔ Don't leave containers of water—even toilet bowls—uncovered. (The parakeet might drown.)

➔ Remove any sharp objects, like nails or needles. (The bird could injure itself.)

➔ Move poisonous house plants to another room. (The parakeet will nibble on them.)

➔ Conceal any electrical wires or cables. (If the bird chews on them, it will be electrocuted.)

➔ Turn off stove burners, extinguish candles (to protect the parakeet against burns).

Clever Oscar

Oscar was in no hurry to hatch into the world. He was the last of three chicks to peck his way out of his shell. The other two birds soon grew big and strong, but Oscar was small and frail. We worried about him. We fed him extra rations of fresh food, and twice a week we added an egg yolk, cooked and chopped fine, mixed with low-fat cottage cheese—his "power meal."

But Oscar soon came into his own. Although he was smaller than the other parakeets, he was not to be outdone in quick-wittedness. Again and again, he astonished us with his endless creativity.

In next to no time, he had discovered how to use the leaves of the yucca plant as a sliding board. Perching where the leaf joined the plant, he would lift his feet in the air and sail—whoosh!—down the leaf. When the kitchen faucet began to drip, he adopted it as his personal shower, spreading his wings and turning himself about with eyes half-closed in pleasure.

Of course, Oscar couldn't read, but he did love his daily newspaper. He would nibble at the edge and tear off little strips. One day, he even made confetti out of a $20 bill that I had carelessly left on the counter.

Oscar lived to be 14 years old—a long life for a parakeet—and he made the most of every minute, in his own special way.

←OSCAR

Fun and Games

More than anything else, Max loves to play.
His favorite toy is this wheel made of sisal cord.
Young parakeets are especially playful, and males more than females. It's important to offer your birds a variety of toys.
Eventually they will select one or more favorites.

with Parakeets

Build an Adventure Playground

Offer your parakeets an ever-changing variety of opportunities to explore, climb, and play.

1 Outside perch

You can buy a perch like this at the pet store. It attaches to the roof of the cage.

2 Seesaw

This plastic seesaw extends from the bars of the cage. As the bird hops from one side to the other, the bells jingle merrily.

3 Fruit kabob

Fruit and vegetable pieces speared on a skewer and fastened to the outside perch or the climbing tree entertain your parakeets with a healthy snack.

4 Climbing tree made of natural branches

Buy this at the pet store, or build your own. Ladders, balls, a seed-encrusted heart, and raffia cord add appeal to the "bird tree."

An Adventure Playground for Parakeets

Parakeets are intelligent and inquisitive. They will explore anything with their beak and tongue, and if possible they'll take it apart. This applies equally to the carpet on the floor and the gripping whodunit that you haven't quite finished, but that now lies in shreds before you. That's why it's a good idea to provide your parakeets with their own playground. The photo below shows how easy it is to put together a mini-entertainment center for your parakeets. They can climb and balance to their hearts' content on the swinging rope; a few knots add to the fun. A bundle of grain stalks, tied with raffia cord, gives them something to tug and nibble at. Even the clothespins will be carefully inspected. The bright wooden beads—actually a child's toy—are varnished with nontoxic dye. Parakeets see in vivid color, so this toy is especially stimulating. And besides, it rattles so nicely when they work it over with their beaks.

A playground for swinging, nibbling, climbing, tugging, rattling, and exploring.

What Sort of Games Does Your Parakeet Like?

Animals play in different ways—with games that focus on objects, movement, partner play, and competition. Observe your parakeets and keep track of the kind of games each bird enjoys. This will help you to understand them better.

	YES	NO
1 Likes to pick up objects in its beak and drop them.	○	○
2 Often swings on ropes and branches.	○	○
3 Plays with wooden beads threaded on a rod.	○	○
4 Young parakeets chase each other around the room.	○	○
5 Plays follow-the-leader through a dark tunnel.	○	○
6 Likes to tug with its beak on the end of a branch, cord, or feather.	○	○
7 Clutches the perch with its claws and tumbles forward (half somersault).	○	○
8 Collects and plays with pens and pencils.	○	○
9 Young male parakeets engage in friendly tussles.	○	○
10 Pushes a wad of paper around with its beak.	○	○

Key: Your parakeet prefers the following types of play, depending on which games you checked "yes":
Object: Games 1, 3, 8, and 10.
Movement: Games 2 and 7.
Competition: Games 6 and 9.
Partners: Games 4 and 5.

Parakeets Need to Play

Very few species of animals play, for play is a perilous undertaking. Immersed in play and oblivious to its surroundings, the animal is vulnerable to predators. Only animals with a well-developed brain—and these include parakeets—can enjoy the luxury of play. However, playing is by no means an extravagance of nature. Animals with a large brain use play in their youth to absorb and process an enormous amount of information. As they play, they learn about their own skills and strengths and those of their playmates. Games provide practice for the serious work of later life; for higher animals, therefore, play is a necessity. Be sure to shower your parakeets with opportunities for play.

Playing and thinking go hand in hand. Offer your parakeets mental challenges as well (see page 50). The best incentive is food. However, don't force your parakee if they are unwilling to play along. Parakeets ca play only when they are completely relaxed an free of fear. To lessen their natural timidity, t a tempting sprig of fresh greenery to the to you want them to explore. Food and curiosi increase the desire to play.

A Few Tips About Play

1. Parakeets are often especially frolicsome the morning and the evening.

2. Tame parakeets also will play with human Gently roll a ball of yarn toward your little budd Don't worry, he won't be alarmed; rather, he w boldly tackle the ball with his beak, or unwind and nibble at the yarn.

3. A particularly tame parakeet, intrigued by th pen or pencil you're writing with, may hop rigl onto your hand for an exploratory nibble. If yo hold your hand in a horizontal position (pal down) and move it quickly up and down, the bir will take off and land again in rhythm. See ho

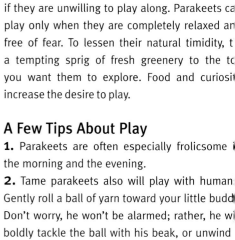

Parakeets enjoy a game just as much as children do.

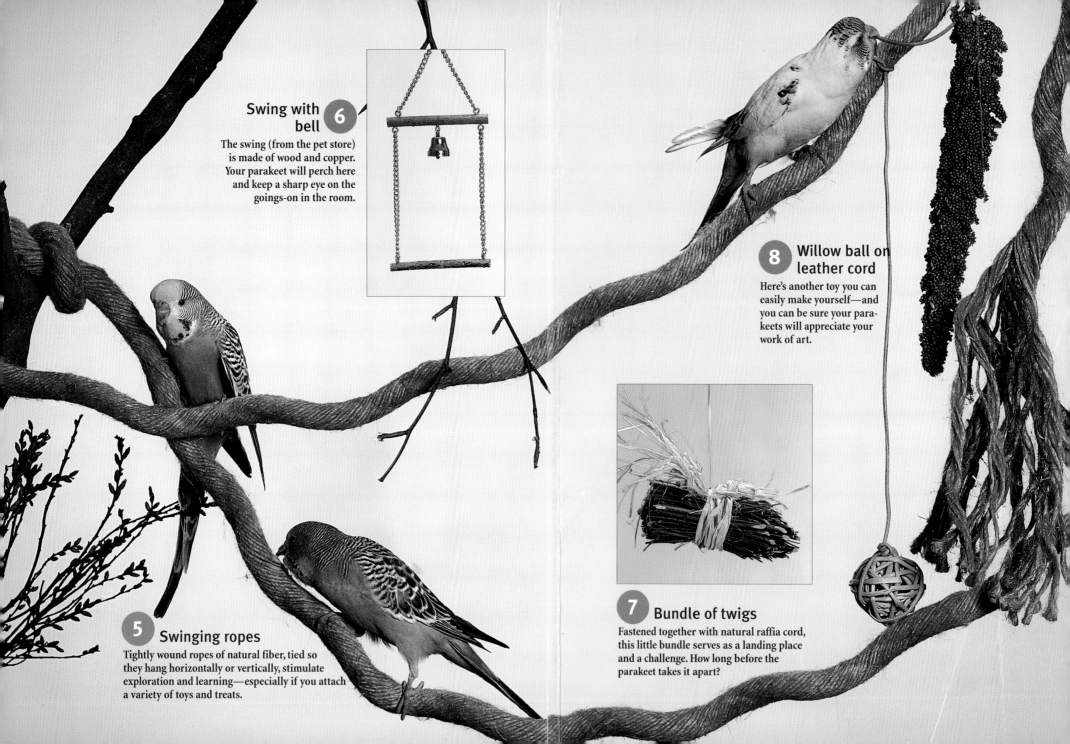

Swing with bell 6

The swing (from the pet store) is made of wood and copper. Your parakeet will perch here and keep a sharp eye on the goings-on in the room.

8 Willow ball on leather cord

Here's another toy you can easily make yourself—and you can be sure your parakeets will appreciate your work of art.

5 Swinging ropes

Tightly wound ropes of natural fiber, tied so they hang horizontally or vertically, stimulate exploration and learning—especially if you attach a variety of toys and treats.

7 Bundle of twigs

Fastened together with natural raffia cord, this little bundle serves as a landing place and a challenge. How long before the parakeet takes it apart?

How Happy Is Your Parakeet?

For how many minutes a day does your parakeet chirp or sing?

- ( ) None — *0 points*
- ( ) 10 minutes — *1 point*
- ( ) More — *2 points*

How many hours a day can your parakeet fly freely about?

- ( ) None — *0 points*
- ( ) 1 hour — *1 point*
- ( ) More — *3 points*

Does it take advantage of the opportunity for flight?

- ( ) Yes — *3 points*
- ( ) No — *0 points*

Does the bird fly about with its mate?

- ( ) Yes — *3 points*
- ( ) No — *0 points*

How do its feathers look?

- ( ) Shiny — *2 points*
- ( ) Dull — *0 points*

Do your parakeets groom each other's head and neck?

- ( ) Never — *0 points*
- ( ) Rarely — *1 point*
- ( ) Often — *3 points*

Whom does the bird try to feed with food from its crop?

- ( ) You — *0 points*
- ( ) The mirror — *0 points*
- ( ) Its mate — *3 points*

How do the parakeets react when you approach?

- ( ) Fly away — *0 points*
- ( ) Shrink back — *1 point*
- ( ) Sit still — *2 points*

How often does the bird preen its feathers?

- ( ) Every day — *3 points*
- ( ) Every other day — *1 point*
- ( ) Never — *0 points*

Does the bird sit in its cage, flapping its wings?

- ( ) Yes — *0 points*
- ( ) No — *3 points*
- ( ) Sometimes — *0 points*

How does the parakeet react to new offerings, such as twigs and branches?

- ( ) Shies away — *0 points*
- ( ) Looks at them — *1 point*
- ( ) Nibbles at them — *3 points*

0–10 points: This is not a happy parakeet. **10–18 points:** Things could be better. **18–25 points:** Good, but not great. **25–30 points:** All's right with the world.

A Mental Challenge

The other day, I gave my little flock of six parakeets a mental challenge. On a stool in the middle of the room I set a birdcage they had never seen before. On top of the cage, I placed a spray of millet. Then I removed all the other food from their indoor aviary. At first the birds were wary of the unfamiliar cage, but soon they grew bolder, and before long they had gathered around the millet for a sociable snack. So far, the challenge wasn't so difficult. But next I took the millet spray from their midst and placed it inside the cage, in plain sight. I left a cage door open. When the parakeets landed on top of the cage again, hoping to resume their nibbling, the snack was no longer there. Soon, though, they spied it inside the cage. I watched as they tried to figure out how to get at the tasty tidbit. After a while, a few gave up and flew away, but the more clever parakeets per-sisted until they discovered the open door. In no time, they had found their way inside and were pecking with gusto at their prize. Was it just coincidence that they had solved the puzzle? I didn't think so, be-cause when I repeated the exercise, opening a different door, the same parakeets caught on to the trick right away. The others were too timid, or perhaps just not interested in playing my little game.

your feathered friend delights in the sensation of motion and speed.

4. Mirrors and shiny metal surfaces are generally not suitable toys. A male parakeet might be confused or intimidated by his reflection. Some parakeets, however, may actually enjoy looking at themselves.

Can Parakeets Learn to Talk?

Parakeets are true artists of mimicry, and some can learn to imitate human speech. If you try repeating a few sentences in a language that's totally unfamiliar to you, you'll have some idea of what a difficult mental process this involves. Even so, a few rare geniuses of the species can rattle off more than 300 sentences, 500 words, and eight children's songs. But this accomplishment comes at great cost, for parakeets learn to talk only when they grow up in isolation from other parakeets. In my opinion, this is too high a price to pay.

TIP from the PET STORE

To keep your parakeets entertained and mentally challenged, rotate their toys so they always have something new to play with. Swings with bells are popular, as are hollow balls with bright rattles inside. You can even make your own toys from natural twigs and branches, raffia twine, and assorted tasty treats.

Although parakeets are attracted to anything that gleams or sparkles, a mirror may not be an appropriate toy for some parakeets.

Active and Happ

Toby, pictured at right, is just six weeks old, while Tuffer is already seven years old—a senior citizen. But the young parakeet and the old one get along just fine. To be sure, Tuffer can't quite keep up with Toby's aerial acrobatics, and he doesn't chirp as loudly or as long. But the two pals often perch contentedly side by side, grooming each other or sharing a midmorning snack.

in Old Age

old & happy

How Long Do Parakeets Live?

On average, parakeets live to be 14 to 16 years old. My cockatiel is still thriving at 30, while cockatoos, the larger cousins of the cockatiel, can even live to be 100 years old.

Among mammals, humans are the species that live the longest. We take this for granted, but biologists still ask why the life span of humans extends far beyond the length of time it takes for parents to rear their own offspring. One possible answer lies in the children themselves. Human babies need a great deal of care for many years, and grandparents are a big help to the parents.

By contrast, most animals live only as long as they are still capable of reproducing. My 30-year-old cockatiel continues to mate with his much younger partner. Thus, the aging process of humans and animals is fundamentally different.

Very old animals are seldom seen in the wild, because older animals are easy prey.

The Golden Years

➜ Behavior:

With age, the parakeets chirp and sing less; they become less curious and more timid about novelty.

➜ Diet:

Older birds need the same amount of food. Unfamiliar food usually is not accepted.

➜ Feathers:

The plumage retains its accustomed sheen; the parakeet may molt less often.

➜ Hygiene:

Older parakeets don't have the strength to groom themselves as often as they used to. You should take care that their bottoms are kept clean.

➜ Motion:

Aging parakeets fly more slowly and fly less. Their movements may be awkward.

➜ Vision:

We don't know whether older birds have less keen vision. To me, it seems unlikely.

➜ Hearing:

It's also not known whether a parakeet's hearing declines with age.

➜ Health:

Most parakeets don't seem to have age-related problems such as arthritis. On the other hand, many birds die of tumors.

How to Recognize an Older Parakeet

Not only humans, but also animals show the effects of aging. These are more obvious in dogs and cats than in birds, but if you observe your parakeets carefully, you also will be able to detect the signs of old age. In males, the blue cere above the beak often turns brownish as the parakeet grows old. Aging birds typically also become less agile in flight. While juvenile parakeets find it fun to detour around obstacles, older birds find this increasingly difficult. They prefer a short, direct

rest only to groom each other, billing and cooing as in their younger days. Only their slower and more awkward movements betray their age.

The bond between a pair of parakeets endures for life, even if one of the partners is considerably younger. The difference in age apparently does not concern them. From the biological standpoint, this fidelity is difficult to explain. Perhaps the enduring bond between mates is found only in domesticated parakeets and not among their relatives in the wild. We still don't know for sure.

flight path, and they seek to conserve their strength.

Not unlike humans in their later years, aging parakeets need a familiar environment. Their feed and water dishes should always be kept in the same spot and readily accessible. Older birds take pleasure in the sun's warmth, and a pair will often perch for hours side by side, dozing in the sunshine. They rouse from their

Even older parakeets need a daily period of free flight.

TIP from the VETERINARIAN

As a parakeet gets older, changes in its metabolism may cause its claws or beak to grow too long. This makes it hard for the bird to climb and eat. Take the parakeet to the veterinarian to have the claws or beak trimmed.

Age brings little change in the eating habits of parakeets. They continue to prefer the same foods they ate as young birds, except that they may eat less in the way of greens. There is no need to adjust the food you offer to your older parakeets.

You will notice that older parakeets chirp and sing less than younger ones. Again, the reason is to conserve energy. In my experience, very old birds also molt less often, or not at all.

Many of the typical age-related illnesses we see in humans and many other mammals do not occur in parakeets.

How Parakeets Die

The life of most birds hangs from a much more slender thread than that of mammals. A parakeet's rate of metabolism is much higher than that of a dog or cat. Metabolic disorders that may cause a dog or cat to gradually decline in health can be fatal in a parakeet. The sudden death of a pet parakeet can be a sad blow, but we can console ourselves that it spares the little bird a long period of suffering. Perhaps even for us, who have enjoyed the company of our feathered friends for many years, their swift departure makes it easier to say good-bye.

But how do parakeets die? Here again, very few scientific studies have been done. I can only speak from my own experience. A parakeet that is near death will leave its perch and huddle in a corner of the cage, dozing deeply and breathing heavily. I have never seen a bird struggle with death throes, as some humans do. Death seems to come easily and swiftly, within a few hours at most. Even very old birds don't seem to suffer, unless they have a tumor—one of the most common causes of death. Usually it is not necessary to have the veterinarian end a parakeet's life, but if your parakeet develops a tumor that seriously impairs its quality of life, you should consult your veterinarian about the options for relieving its misery.

Mourning Your Pet

The death of a beloved pet is a sad occasion. Many pet owners are surprised at the intensity of their own grief. But these feelings must be respected, rather than lightly dismissed. When we grieve at the death of a pet, we are mourning a living creature that was a part of our lives, brought sparkle to our days and laughter to our hearts. Our pet was a companion, a comrade, a dear friend. Though people mourned for animals in times past as well, in today's world the relationship between humans and their pets is often an especially close one. Unfortunately, in modern society we also are reluctant to talk about death and grief, especially when it was "only" a pet that died.

And how do children and teenagers respond? The death of a pet is often their first experience of saying good-bye forever. The impression it makes will be deep and unforgettable. For this reason, it's important to be especially

understanding with children whose pet has died. Listen to them carefully and take their feelings seriously.

Death is a part of life, but this fact is difficult for anyone to comprehend, and even more so for children. A simple and sympathetic explanation of why the pet died can ease the pain of parting. Finally, children naturally are concerned that the

Many parakeets delight in music. These two can't get enough of hearing "their" human play.

animal's final journey should be a dignified one. Their faithful friend deserves respect, even after death. Help them to bury the parakeet's body in a peaceful resting place.

When a Parakeet Loses Its Mate

What are the feelings of a parakeet when its mate dies? Of course, we don't know for sure, but judging from their behavior, the sudden loss and loneliness must be terrible. Many parakeets call out for their mates over and over and over; others become listless and just sit there in the cage. To bring an end to this sad situation, you should introduce the bereaved parakeet to another companion after a period of time. It doesn't matter whether the new parakeet is the same age. Even if one of them is much younger, the parakeets will get along fine. Naturally, you must give them time to get to know each other. This isn't always easy, because at first the older bird might attack the newcomer. Follow the procedures described on page 35, and before long your parakeets should be fast friends.

Age and youth can forge a friendship, and not only between parakeets; a child and an older parakeet can also be pals.

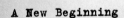

A New Beginning

One morning, we found our dear parakeet
Tillie lying still on the floor of the cage.
She had died during the night. For 12 years,
she had been a part of our lives—sitting on my
shoulder and chatting away, or nibbling tenderly
at my ear during her daily outing. Gently, I took
her little body from the cage while Jake, her
mate, huddled in the far corner. We buried Tillie
in the garden, under a beautiful apple tree. We
consoled ourselves that at least we still had
Jake, but when we returned to the house, no
friendly twitter greeted us. Jake was a bundle of
misery. None of our coaxing and pampering would
restore his usual good cheer. After a few days,
we were really worried. What could we do to
comfort Jake? We decided that he needed a new
companion. That day, we brought home a young
female parakeet we named Dolly. Sure enough, our
plan worked. Jake didn't exactly welcome her at
first, but before long he began to respond to her
timid chirps and warbles, and now Jake
is happy as can be with his little
Dolly.

Index

Dr. Immanuel Birmelin
is an internationally respected behavioral biologist. His many years of research, documented in numerous publications and on television, have yielded much new information about animals and their behavior.

Monika Wegler
is one of the leading animal photographers in Europe. She is also a journalist and an author of books about animals. She took all the photographs in this book except the one on page 14, which was taken by Arendt/Schweiger.

Gabriele Linke-Grün
has worked for many years as a freelance writer for the Gräfe und Unzer nature book series and for various animal magazines and textbook publishers. She wrote our *Parakeet Stories*.

This perky fellow
seems quite at ease.

Useful Books

Other bird titles published by Barron's Educational Series, Inc. include:

Birmelin, Immanuel, *Budgerigars: A Complete Pet Owner's Manual*, 1998.

Birmelin, Immanuel and Annette Wolter, *The Parakeet Handbook*, 2000.

Burgmann, Petra, *Feeding Your Pet Bird*, 1993.

Dorenkamp, Bernard, *Natural Health Care for Your Bird*, 1998.

Freud, Arthur, *Parakeets: A Complete Pet Owner's Manual*, 1999.

Viner, Bradley, *All About Your Budgerigar*, 1998.

Wolter, Annette, *Budgerigars: Family Pet Series*, 1997.

——, *Long-Tailed Parakeets: A Complete Pet Owner's Manual*, 1992.

Wolter, Annette and Monika Wegler, *The Complete Book of the Parakeet*, 1994.

Acknowledgments

The photographer and the publisher wish to thank the firm Wagner & Keller of Ludwigshafen, Germany, for its gracious support. The company has worked successfully for many years to promote suitable conditions in bird and animal shelters.

English translation © Copyright 2001 by Barron's Educational Series, Inc.

Original title of the book in German is *Mein Wellensittich und ich* Copyright © 2000 by Grafe und Unzer Verlag GmbH, Munich

Translation from the German by Celia Bohannon

All inquiries should be addressed to:
Barron's Educational Series, Inc.
250 Wireless Boulevard
Hauppauge, New York 11788
http://www.barronseduc.com

Library of Congress Catalog Card No. 00-106409

International Standard Book No. 0-7641-1807-2

Printed in Hong Kong

9 8 7 6 5 4 3 2 1